THE FUNNIEST QUOTATIONS TO BRIGHTEN EVERY DAY

Brilliant, Inspiring, and Hilarious Thoughts from Great Minds

Heeheehee...

Edited by Team Golfwell & Bruce Miller J.D.

Published by Pacific Trust Holdings NZ Ltd.

The Funniest Quotations to Brighten Every Day by Team Golfwell

The Funniest Quotations to Brighten Every Day: Brilliant, Inspiring, and Hilarious Thoughts from Great Minds, Copyright © 2019, Pacific Trust Holdings NZ, Ltd. All rights reserved. All content in this book (including text, translations, graphics, categories, systems, and any improvements or modifications to such content; and any derivative works) is the property of Team Golfwell.

All quotations remain the intellectual property of their respective originators. We do not assert any claim of copyright for individual quotations. All use of quotations is done under the fair use copyright principal.

The collection, arrangement and assembly of content of this book is the exclusive property of Team Golfwell and Bruce Miller and are likewise protected by copyright and other intellectual property laws.

Image is from Creative Commons

The Funniest Quotations to Brighten Every Day by Team Golfwell

Table of Contents

Introduction 1

Advice 3

Alcohol 6

Appreciation 9

Arguments 11

Assumptions 14

Astrology 17

Beauty 20

Being Yourself 24

Bullies 26

Celebrities 28

Children 30

Church 34

Computers 36

The Funniest Quotations to Brighten Every Day by Team Golfwell

Confidence 38

Criticism 40

Dads 42

Dating 46

Divorce 50

Dogs 52

Driving 54

Doctors 56

Education 58

Employment 61

Enemies 63

Environment 65

Failure 68

Family 70

Fashion 74

Flattery 77

Food 79

Free Speech 82

Friends 84

Future 87

Gay 89

Genius 93

Happiness 95

Hate 97

Health 98

Heaven 100

Humor 101

Insanity 106

Irony 108

Know It Alls 111

Lawyers 113

Laziness 115

Lies 116

Life 117

Love 123

Man's Best Friend 125

Marriage 127

Materialism 133

Men 135

Mistakes 139

Mothers 142

Motivation 146

Music 148

Offended 150

Old Age 151

Opportunities 156

Optomism 157

Overweight 159

Parents 161

Perfection 164

Pessimists 166

Phones 167

Politics 169

Procrastination 172

Psychics 174

Skeletons in the closet ... 176

Sex 177

Sports 179

Teens 182

Truth 185

The Funniest Quotations to Brighten Every Day by Team Golfwell

Trust 186
Women 187
Work 193
World 195
About the Editors 199

Introduction

From #1 Bestselling Authors on Amazon, Team Golfwell and Bruce Miller J.D. bring you a timeless collection of some of the funniest, brilliant and inspiring thoughts to brighten your day. You can pick this book up anytime for your own amusement and enjoyment to find an intriguing or funny quote to assist your presentation or speech, or make a family member, or a friend happy, motivated and inspired with the right words.

This book is an excellent source for the right thing to say at the right time for people in sales, sales managers, writers and speechwriters, students or anyone wanting to focus and deeply relate to people.

Laughter has a way of brightening your day and cheering you on. Laughter has been scientifically proven to be healthy and relaxing. Laughter makes clients and people around you more receptive and open.

The Funniest Quotations to Brighten Every Day by Team Golfwell

The wisdom, cheer and humor of these quotes will tend to make people pause and listen when you're speaking.

This book is also a good source for anyone when they simply need basic, good and funny advice.

All quotes are arranged alphabetically by subject.

The hundreds of poignant and funny quotations all spaced well apart for reflection and personal notes in the paperback edition.

The eBook is convenient to have on your phone to access anytime.

The Book of Quotes will keep you intrigued, motivated, recharged, and ready to deal with the world we live in with new clarity, energy and focus.

We hope you enjoy it and these amazing quotations benefit you and all those around you!

Advice

Listen, everyone is entitled to my opinion. – *Madonna*

The one thing you shouldn't do is try to tell a cab driver how to get somewhere. *- Jimmy Fallon*

Never under any circumstances take a sleeping pill and a laxative on the same night. – *Dave Barry*

A great pleasure in life is doing what people say you cannot do. – *Walter Bagehot*

Everybody knows how to raise children, except the people who have them. *- P. J. O'Rourke*

Good advice is something a man gives when he is too old to set a bad example.
– Francois de La Rochefoucauld

The advice I would give to someone is to not take anyone's advice. - Eddie Murphy

Never take advice about never taking advice. That is an old vice of men - to dish it out without being able to take it - the blind leading the blind into more blindness. - Criss Jami, Healology

Everyone's got skeletons in their closet, and I've got a million in mine, believe me. I tested the envelope; I pushed it. Whenever somebody in authority told me not to do something, I did it just to find out why they said not to do it. - Denis Leary

Some advice: No matter what people tell you; words and ideas can change the world. - *Robin Williams*

The best advice comes from people who don't give advice. - *Matthew McConaughey*

The best advice I've ever received is, 'No one else knows what they're doing either'. - *Ricky Gervais*

Of course, I talk to myself. Sometimes I need an expert opinion. – *Bill Murray*

Alcohol

I believe that if life gives you lemons, you should make lemonade... And try to find somebody whose life has given them vodka and have a party. – *Ron White*

Alcohol is like Photoshop for real life. - *Will Ferrell*

Wine is constant proof that God loves us and loves to see us happy. – *Benjamin Franklin*

Alcohol is the anesthesia by which we endure the operation of life. - *George Bernard Shaw*

I drink to make other people more interesting. – *Ernest Hemingway*

Always carry a flagon of whiskey in case of snakebite and furthermore always carry a small snake. – *W. C. Fields*

I used to jog but the ice cubes kept falling out of my glass. – *David Lee Roth*

If you drink anymore, you're going to spill and be positively flammable. - *Michaela Haze*

When I read about the evils of drinking, I gave up reading. - *Henny Youngman*

The simple act of opening a bottle of wine has brought more happiness to the

human race than all the collective governments in the history of earth. – *Jim Harrison*

One tequila, two tequila, three tequila, floor. – *George Carlin*

An alcoholic is someone you don't like who drinks as much as you do. – *Dylan Thomas*

Age is just a number. It's totally irrelevant unless, of course, you happen to be a bottle of wine. – *Joan Collins*

Give a man a fish and he will have food for one day. Teach him to catch fish and he will spend all day at the lake drinking beer. – *Anon.*

Appreciation

You will have bad times, but the bad times will always wake you up to the stuff you weren't paying attention to (and appreciate it a lot more). - *Robin Williams*

Don't cry because it's over. Smile because it happened. – *Dr. Seuss*

As we express our gratitude, we must never forget that the highest appreciation is not to utter words, but to live by them. - *John F. Kennedy*

If you are thankful for what you have; you'll end up having more. If you concentrate on what you don't have, you will never, ever have enough. - *Oprah Winfrey*

Forget yesterday - it has already forgotten you. Don't sweat tomorrow - you haven't even met. Instead, open your eyes and your heart to a truly precious gift - today. - *Steve Maraboli*

I'm trying to develop an attitude of gratitude, but the best I can muster up is a sentiment of resentment. – *Randy Glasbergen*

My socks may not match, but my feet are always warm. - *Maureen McCullough*

If a fellow isn't thankful for what he's got, he isn't likely to be thankful for what he's going to get. - *Frank A. Clark*

Arguments

I'm not arguing. I'm simply explaining why I'm right. – *Anon.*

My favorite comedians are just presenting an argument, and they're doing it in a funny way. - *Hasan Minhaj*

Try to find someone with a sense of humor. That's an important thing to have because when you get into an argument, one of the best ways to diffuse it is to be funny.

You don't want to hide away from a point, because some points are serious, but you'd rather have a discussion that was a discussion, rather than an argument. - *Ed Sheeran*

I guess when I think about it, one of the things I like to dramatize, and what is sometimes funny, is someone coming unglued. I don't consider myself someone who is making the argument that I support these choices. I just think it can be funny. - *Wes Anderson*

My life is my argument. - *Albert Schweitzer*

Behind every argument is someone's ignorance. - *Louis D. Brandeis*

Arguments are healthy. They clear the air. - *John Deacon*

**"You got something you wanna say to me?" is a way of opening the door for someone brooding to let the feelings out. – *Anon*.

The moment we want to believe something, we suddenly see all the arguments for it, and become blind to the arguments against it. - *George Bernard Shaw*

Answer not a fool according to his folly, lest thou also be like unto him – *Proverbs (26:4)*

Arguing with anonymous strangers on the Internet is a sucker's game because they almost always turn out to be—or to be indistinguishable from—self-righteous sixteen-year-olds possessing infinite amounts of free time. - *Neal Stephenson, Cryptonomicon*

Assumptions

It is impossible for a man to learn what he assumes and thinks he already knows. – *Epictetus*

I don't care what is written about me as long as it isn't true. - *Katherine Hepburn*

In general, the straight line of a joke sets up a premise, an expectation. Then the funny ending - the punch line - in a sense contradicts the original assumption by refusing to follow what had seemed a reasonable train of thought. Many jokes involve that simple matter of leaping outside what had appeared to be the rules of the game at the moment. - *Steve Allen*

Begin challenging your own assumptions. Your assumptions are

your windows on the world. Scrub them off every once in a while, or the light won't come in. - *Alan Alda*

When we believe in lies, we cannot see the truth, so we make thousands of assumptions and we take them as truth. One of the biggest assumptions we make is that the lies we believe are the truth! - *Don Miguel Ruiz*

Wethern's Law of suspended judgment: Assumption is the mother of all screw-ups. – *Murphy's Law*

The harder you fight to hold on to specific assumptions, the more likely there's gold in letting go of them. - *John Seely Brown*

You must stick to your conviction but be ready to abandon your assumptions. - *Denis Waitley*

The creative individual has the capacity to free himself from the web of social pressures in which the rest of us are caught. He is capable of questioning the assumptions that the rest of us accept. - *John W. Gardner*

Dearest husband, if I am overly irritable please don't "assume" I am having my period ... otherwise, when you are sleeping, I may just "assume" you are dead and bury you in the backyard. – *Anon.*

Astrology

I don't believe in astrology; I'm a Sagittarius and we're skeptical. - *Arthur C. Clark*

About astrology and palmistry: they are good because they make people vivid and full of possibilities. They are communism at its best. Everybody has a birthday and almost everybody has a palm. - *Kurt Vonnegut*

A short excerpt from Good Omens: The Nice and Accurate Prophecies of Agnes Nutter, Witch:

"Archbishop James Usher (1580-1656) published Annales Veteris et Novi Testaments in 1654, which suggested that the Heaven and the Earth were created in 4004 B.C. One of his aides took the calculation further and was able to announce triumphantly that the

Earth was created on Sunday the 21st of October, 4004 B.C., at exactly 9:00 A.M., because God liked to get work done early in the morning while he was feeling fresh.

This too was incorrect. By almost a quarter of an hour.

The whole business with the fossilized dinosaur skeletons was a joke the paleontologists haven't seen yet.

This proves two things:

Firstly, that God moves in extremely mysterious, not to say, circuitous ways. God does not play dice with the universe; He plays an ineffable game of His own devising, which might be compared, from the perspective of any of the other players, (i.e., everybody) to being involved in an obscure and complex version of poker in a pitch-dark room, with blank cards, for infinite stakes, with a Dealer who won't tell you the rules, and who smiles all the time.

Secondly, the Earth's a Libra." - *Terry Pratchett,*

"Correct." Kekrops sounded bitter, like he regretted his decision. "My people were the original Athenians--the Gemini."

"Like your zodiac sign?" Percy asked. "I'm a Leo."

"No, stupid," Leo said. "I'm a Leo. You're a Percy."

— *Rick Riordan, The Blood of Olympus*

Beauty

Smiling is definitely one of the best beauty remedies. If you have a good sense of humor and a good approach to life, that's beautiful. - *Rashida Jones*

I think beauty comes from actually knowing who you are. That's real beauty to me. - *Ellen DeGeneres*

Weak eyebrows equal weak presentation. It's like having a bad handshake, but worse because it's right on your face. - *Lena Dunham, from Not That Kind of Girl*

If you retain nothing else, always remember the most important Rule of Beauty, which is: "Who cares?" - *Tina Fey, from Bossypants*

I have no illusions about my looks. I think my face is funny. - *Audrey Hepburn*

Who is the beauty icon that inspires you the most? Is it Sophia Loren? Audrey Hepburn? Halle Berry? Mine is Nosferatu, because that vampire taught me my number-one and number-two favorite beauty tricks of all time: avoid the sun at all costs and always try to appear shrouded in shadows. —*Mindy Kaling*

Maybe you should eat some makeup so you can be pretty on the inside too. – *Anon.*

If you're hotter than me, then that means I'm cooler than you. – *Anon.*

"At last I'm old enough to know that the collective points of view on what is beautiful will always be subject to the vicissitudes and whims of a generation. So will our own faces and bodies change over the course of a lifetime...

The things that I find truly beautiful now are more subtle and rare but can access a depth of emotion that I didn't even know existed in me. My mother's hands scarred from years of pruning her own garden. The nape of my daughter's neck. My son's eyebrows inherited from his grandfather. A selected line of a Mary Oliver poem. The way my husband looks at me as he enters our bed after we've survived another long day. My vanishing freckles." - *Molly Ringwald, from "The Cute One," Allure, March 2014*

I'm baffled that anyone might not think women get more beautiful as they get

older. Confidence comes with age and looking beautiful comes from the confidence someone has in themselves.
- Kate Winslet

There is nothing more rare, nor more beautiful, than a woman being unapologetically herself; comfortable in her perfect imperfection. To me, that is the true essence of beauty. - *Steve Maraboli*

There are no bad pictures; that's just how your face looks sometimes. - *Abraham Lincoln*

Being Yourself

There's a wonderful sense of well-being that begins to circulate… up and down your spine. And you feel something that makes you almost want to smile.

So, what's it like to be me? Ask yourself, 'What's it like to be me?' The only way we'll ever know what it's like to be you is if you work your best at being you as often as you can and keep reminding yourself that's where home is. - *Bill Murray*

Be who you are and say what you feel, because those who mind don't matter and those who matter don't mind. – *Bernard Baruch*

Be yourself; everyone else is already taken. - *Oscar Wilde*

I used to think I was indecisive, but now I'm not too sure. – *Anon.*

To be yourself in a world that is constantly trying to make you something else is the greatest accomplishment. - *Ralph Waldo Emerson*

Imperfection is beauty, madness is genius and it's better to be yourself and be absolutely ridiculous than absolutely boring. - *Marilyn Monroe*

We're all pretty bizarre. Some of us are just better at hiding it, that's all. - *John Hughes, The Breakfast Club*

Bullies

People who love themselves, don't hurt other people. The more we hate ourselves, the more we want others to suffer. - *Dan Pearce*

One of the greatest pieces of advice I've ever gotten in my life was from my mom. When I was a little kid there was a kid who was bugging me at school and she said "Okay, I'm gonna tell you what to do. If the kid's bugging you and puts his hands on you; you pick up the nearest rock... - *Johnny Depp*

Everyone who wants to do good to the human race always ends in universal bullying. - *Aldous Huxley*

**When all of us are acknowledged as the human equals that we really are, there

will be no space left for bullying. It will no longer be wrong to choose one thing over another. -*Jason Mraz*

If people are trying to bring you down, it only means you are above them. – *Anon.*

You always have to remember that bullies want to bring you down because you have something that they admire. Also, when you get made fun of - when people point out your weaknesses, it's an opportunity for you to rise above. - *Zac Efron*

Never be bullied into silence. Never allow yourself to be made a victim. Accept no one's definition of your life; define yourself. - *Harvey Fierstein*

Celebrities

A celebrity is a person who works hard all his life to become well known, then wears dark glasses to avoid being recognized. - *Fred Allen*

Like Andy Warhol and unlike God Almighty, Larry King does not presume to judge; all celebrities are equal in his eyes, saints and sinners alike sharing the same 'Love Boat' voyage into the dark beyond, a former sitcom star as deserving of pious send-off as Princess Diana. - *James Wolcott*

We want to talk to celebrities about the thing's celebrities don't normally talk about. Like, we'd love to get Kim Kardashian to talk to us about finance. She is a businesswoman, after all. - *Jennifer Konner*

Social media lacks insight, common sense, and emotion. Understand that while it's easy to condemn celebrities on social media, people should also think of repercussions their insensitive remarks can make on the celebrities' family. - *Neil Nitin Mukesh*

I don't like talking to celebrities. – *Lady Gaga*

I kind of understand now why people freak out when they see celebrities that they love, because that's how I feel about every single Muppet. - *Rashida Jones*

Children

If you want your children to listen, try talking softly to someone else. - *Ann Landers*

Cleaning up with children around is like shoveling during a blizzard. – *Margaret Culkin Banning*

Never have more children than you have car windows. – *Erma Bombeck*

Folks, I don't trust children. They're here to replace us. – *Stephen Colbert*

Having children is like living in a frat house – nobody sleeps, everything's

broken, and there's a lot of throwing up.
- *Ray Romano*

We spend the first twelve months of our children's lives teaching them to walk and talk and the next twelve telling them to sit down and shut up. – *Phyllis Diller*

Everyone should have kids. They are the greatest joy in the world. But they are also terrorists. You'll realize this as soon as they are born and start using sleep deprivation to torture you. - *Ray Romano*

The quickest way for a parent to get a child's attention is to sit down and look comfortable. - *Lane Olinghouse*

I want my children to have all the things I couldn't afford. Then I want to move in with them. – *Phyllis Diller*

It just occurred to me that the majority of my diet is made up of the foods that my kid didn't finish. - *Carrie Underwood*

We never really grow up. We just learn how to act in public. - *Bryan White*

Don't yell at your kids! Lean in real close and whisper, it's much scarier. – *Anon.*

By the time a man realizes that his father was right, he has a son who thinks he's wrong. – *Charles Wadsworth*

My daughter, Hannah, my 7-year-old, lost her first tooth and the tooth fairy came. And then the next day we were taking a video, 'Hey Hannah, the tooth fairy came, oh my gosh,' and our 4-year-old—I panned down to her, 'Hey Harper, the tooth fairy came!'

And she goes, 'Someone was in our house?'

And I go, 'The tooth fairy was in our house.'

And she's like, "Someone was in my room? While I was sleeping? And you guys are cool with this." - *Bill Hader*

Adults are just outdated children. - *Dr. Seuss*

Children must be taught how to think, not what to think. - *Margaret Mead*

Church

Going to church doesn't make you a Christian any more than going to a garage makes you an automobile. – *Billy Sunday*

When we talk to God, we're praying. When God talks to us, we're schizophrenic. – *Jane Wagner*

In the past 10,000 years, humans have devised roughly 100,000 religions based on roughly 2,500 gods. So, the only difference between myself and the believers is that I am skeptical of 2,500 gods whereas they are skeptical of 2,499 gods. We're only one God away from total agreement. – *Michael Shermer*

The first time I sang in the church choir, two hundred people changed their religion. – *Fred Allen*

I've come to view Jesus much the way I view Elvis. I love the guy, but the fan clubs really freak me out. – *John Fugelsang*

The less Holy Spirit we have, the more cake and coffee we need to keep the church going. – *Reinhard Bonnke*

Computers

A computer once beat me at chess, but it was no match for me at kick boxing. – *Emo Philips*

Computer dating is fine, if you're a computer. – *Anon.*

I went to a gentleman's cybercafe — and they offered me a "laptop dance." – *Anon.*

My wife never gives up. She is so insistent that she entered the wrong password over and over again until she managed to convince the computer that she's right. – *Anon.*

Computer games don't affect kids. I mean if Pac-Man affected us as kids, we'd all be running around in darkened rooms, munching magic pills and listening to repetitive electronic music. - *Marcus Brigstocke*

A child enters your home and for the next twenty years makes so much noise you can hardly stand it. The child departs, leaving the house so silent you think you are going mad. - *John Andrew Holmes*

Confidence

Confidence is what you have before you understand the problem. - *Woody Allen*

To succeed in life, you need two things: ignorance and confidence. - *Mark Twain*

The better you feel about yourself, the less you feel the need to show off. - *Robert Hand*

Think of how stupid the average person is and realize half of them are stupider than that. - *George Carlin*

Confidence is 10% work and 90% delusion. - *Tina Fey*

Until you value yourself, you won't value your time. Until you value your time, you will not do anything with it. – *M. Scott Peck*

Love myself I do. Not everything, but I love the good as well as the bad. I love my crazy lifestyle, and I love my hard discipline. I love my freedom of speech and the way my eyes get dark when I'm tired. I love that I have learned to trust people with my heart, even if it will get broken. I am proud of everything that I am and will become. *- Johnny Weir*

Criticism

People who criticize you have usually never achieved anywhere near what you have. Most of them would be too scared to even try. Keep going. - *Ricky Gervais*

Whenever someone calls me ugly, I get super sad and hug them, because I know how tough life is for the visually impaired. - *Will Ferrell*

Before you criticize a man, walk a mile in his shoes. That way, when you do criticize him, you'll be a mile away and have his shoes. – *Billy Connolly*

**I haven't any right to criticize books, and I don't do it except when I hate them. I often want to criticize Jane Austen, but her books madden me so that I can't conceal my frenzy from the

reader; and therefore, I have to stop every time I begin. Every time I read Pride and Prejudice, I want to dig her up and beat her over the skull with her own shinbone. - *Mark Twain*

Any fool can criticize, condemn, and complain but it takes character and self-control to be understanding and forgiving. – *Dale Carnegie*

When virtues are pointed out first, flaws seem less insurmountable. - *Judith Martin*

Dads

I'm probably the most uncool guy that my daughters know — as far as they are concerned anyway — 'cause I'm Dad.

I mean dads just aren't cool — especially when I dance! They don't want me to dance. - *Tim McGraw*

Twelve weeks old: when your kid is young enough to fall asleep on your chest yet long enough to kick you in the nuts at the same time. - *Lin-Manuel Miranda*

I want to be a dad. That's floating to the top of my list. I think it's such an important thing. I'm at the age where everyone has kids, and I ask them, 'Is it like a puppy?' And they go, 'It's 10 times a puppy.' - *Jimmy Fallon*

I remember the time I was kidnapped, and they sent a piece of my finger to my father. He said he wanted more proof. - *Rodney Dangerfield*

We see a McDonald's. We got so excited. We started chanting, 'McDonald's, McDonald's, McDonald's!' And my dad pulled into the drive thru and we started cheering. And then, he ordered one black coffee for himself... and kept driving. My dad is cold-blooded. *-John Mulaney*

I would say the hardest thing about being a dad or a parent is these goddamn kids. – *Andy Richter*

A father carries pictures where his money used to be. - *Steve Martin*

I think every kid thinks their dad is goofy. Even Johnny Depp's kid must be like, "Oh my god, my dad with those freakin' scarves. This isn't a pirate ship; it's a Costco, dad. - *Judd Apatow*

My daughter got me a 'World's Best Dad' mug. So, we know she's sarcastic. - *Bob Odenkirk*

When I was a boy of 14, my father was so ignorant, I could hardly stand to have the old man around. But when I got to be 21, I was astonished at how much the old man had learned in seven years. - *Mark Twain*

On our 6 a.m. walk, my daughter asked where the moon goes each morning. I let her know it's in heaven visiting daddy's freedom. - *Ryan Reynolds*

I never raised my hand to my kids since it leaves my groin unprotected. - *Red Buttons*

My father gave me the greatest gift anyone could give another person, he believed in me. - *Jim Valvano*

There should be a children's song: 'If you're happy and you know it, keep it to yourself and let your dad sleep.' *-Jim Gaffigan*

Having a kid is like falling in love for the first time when you're 12, but every day. - *Mike Myers*

Dating

What is a date, really, but a job interview that lasts all night? The only difference is that in not many job interviews is there a chance you'll wind up naked. - *Jerry Seinfeld*

When a guy does something stupid once, well that's because he's a guy. But if he does the same stupid thing twice, that's usually to impress some girl. - *The Lorax*

I have always laid it down as a maxim and found it justified by experience - that a man and a woman make far better friendships than can exist between two of the same sex - but then with the condition that they never have made or are to make love to each other. - *Lord Byron*

If you can't live without me, why aren't you dead already? – Cynthia Heimel

Leave something for someone but don't leave someone for something. – Enid Blyton

Failed relationships can be described as so much wasted make-up. - Marian Keyes

Girls only want boyfriends who have great skills. - Napoleon Dynamite

She got really mad a month ago, because she had e-mailed me a naked picture of herself — which is a nice thing to do — but then I messed up, and I accidentally forwarded that e-mail to both of my parents. Now, my girlfriend is furious, mortified, but I don't even

care, 'cause now I have to call up my mother and say 'Mom, I am so sorry — that picture was just for dad.' – *Anthony Jeselnik*

When a man steals your woman there is no better revenge than to let him keep her. - *Sacha Guitry*

A woman who doesn't want to kiss takes her keys out, puts them in the door, goes in the house. A woman that wants to kiss, she fiddles. - *Will Smith, Hitch*

What do I say to her on a date?

A. Just ask a question, that's it. Because women do not care about what you have to say at all and all they want to do is talk about themselves. - *Cal, 40-Year-Old Virgin*

In my opinion, the best thing you can do is find a person who loves you for exactly who you are. Good mood, bad mood, ugly, pretty, handsome... The right person is still going to think the sun shines out of your ass. - *Mac MacGuff, Juno*

Watching your daughter being collected by her date feels like handing over a million-dollar Stradivarius to a gorilla. - *Jim Bishop*

To find a prince, you gotta kiss some toads. - *Foxy Brown*

Divorce

Ah, yes, divorce... from the Latin word meaning to rip out a man's genitals through his wallet. - *Robin Williams*

The only time my wife and I had a simultaneous orgasm was when the judge signed the divorce papers. - *Woody Allen*

A 99-year-old man is filing for divorce from his 96-year-old wife, making them the world's oldest divorced couple. It's got to be weird when a divorce lawyer is fighting for your kids to get custody of you. - *Jimmy Fallon*

Getting divorced just because you don't love a man is almost as silly as getting married just because you do. - *Zsa Zsa Gabor*

I should have known something was wrong with my first wife. When I brought her home to meet my parents, they approved of her. - *Woody Allen*

My divorce came to me as a complete surprise. That's what happens when you haven't been home in eighteen years. - *Lee Trevino*

In every marriage more than a week old, there are grounds for divorce. The trick is to find and continue to find grounds for marriage. - *Robert Anderson*

Dogs

The average dog is a nicer person than the average person. – *Andy Rooney*

The best therapist has fur and four legs. – *Anon.*

If there are no dogs in heaven, then when I die, I want to go where they went. - *Will Rogers*

A dog desires affection more than its dinner. Well – almost. *-Charlotte Gray*

A boy can learn a lot from a dog — obedience, loyalty, and the importance of turning around three times before lying down. – *Robert Benchley*

Ever consider what our dogs must think of us? I mean, here we come back from a grocery store with the most amazing haul, chicken, pork, half a cow. They must think we're the greatest hunters on earth! - *Anne Tyler*

If you think dogs can't count, try putting three dog biscuits in your pocket and then give him only two of them. - *Phil Pastoret*

To err is human - to forgive, canine. - *Anon.*

In the event of a hurricane, fire, avalanche, tornado or other such natural disaster, place dog treats in your pockets so the search dogs can find you first. – *Anon.*

Driving

Have you ever noticed that anybody driving slower than you is an idiot, and anyone going faster than you is a maniac? - *George Carlin*

People that insist upon drinking and driving, are putting the quart before the hearse. - *Gilbert K. Chesterton*

Americans will put up with anything provided it doesn't block traffic. - *Dan Rather*

You know, somebody actually complimented me on my driving today. They left a little note on the windscreen, it said "Parking Fine." - *Tommy Cooper*

I don't sell cars; I sell engines. The cars I throw in for free since something has to hold the engines in. - *Enzo Ferrari*

Of course, in Los Angeles, everything is based on driving, even the killings. In New York, most people don't have cars, so if you want to kill a person, you must take the subway to their house. And sometimes on the way, the train is delayed, and you get impatient, so you have to kill someone on the subway. That's why there are so many subway murders; no one has a car. - *George Carlin, Brain Droppings*

A guy is driving with his wife at his side and his mother-in-law in the backseat. Both women just won't leave him alone.

His mother-in-law says, "You're driving too fast!"

His wife says, "Stay more to the left."

After ten mixed orders, the man turns to his wife and asks, "Who's driving this car – you or your mother?" - *Anon.*

Doctors

Doctors are just the same as lawyers; the only difference is that lawyers merely rob you, whereas doctors rob you and kill you too. - *Anton Chekhov*

An apple a day keeps anyone away if you throw it hard enough. – *Anon.*

Never go to a doctor whose office plants have died. – *Erma Bombeck*

The best doctor gives the least medicines. – *Benjamin Franklin*

Never do anything that you wouldn't want to explain to the doctor. – *Anon.*

My doctor gave me six months to live, but when I couldn't pay the bill, he gave me six months more. – *Walter Matthau*

I told my wife the truth. I told her I was seeing a doctor, a psychiatrist. Then she told me the truth. She was seeing a psychiatrist, two plumbers, and a bartender. - *Rodney Dangerfield*

I told the doctor I broke my leg in two places. He told me to quit going to those places. – *Henny Youngman*

When I told the doctor about my loss of memory, he made me pay in advance. – *Anon.*

Education

Education is a progressive discovery of our own ignorance. - *Will Durant*

It takes considerable knowledge just to realize the extent of your own ignorance. – *Thomas Sowell*

Education is learning what you didn't even know you didn't know. – *Daniel J. Boorstin*

I always thought the idea of education was to learn to think for yourself. - *Robin Williams*

If there are no stupid questions, then what kind of questions do stupid people

ask? Do they get smart just in time to ask questions? – *Scott Adams*

Remember, when you are dead, you do not know you are dead. It is only painful for others. The same applies when you are stupid. *- Ricky Gervais*

A man doesn't know what he knows until he knows what he doesn't know. – *Laurence J. Peter*

In school, you're taught a lesson and then given a test. In life, you're given a test that teaches you a lesson. *- Tom Bodett*

Don't just teach your children to read. Teach them to question what they read,

teach them to question everything. - *George Carlin*

The human brain is special. It starts working as soon as you get up and it doesn't stop until you get to school. - *Milton Berle*

The most important thing we learn at school is the fact that the most important things can't be learned at school. - *Haruki Murakami*

You do not really understand something unless you can explain it to your grandmother. - *Albert Einstein*

Employment

Love what you do. Get good at it. Competence is a rare commodity in this day and age. - *Jon Stewart*

If you spend your days doing what you love, it is impossible to fail. - *Ricky Gervais*

When people ask me how many people work here, I say, about a third of them. - *Lisa Kennedy Montgomery*

I don't want any yes-men around me. I want everybody to tell me the truth even if it costs them their job. – *Samuel Goldwyn*

Oh, you hate your job. Why didn't you say so? There's a support group for that. It's called EVERYBODY, and they meet at the bar. - *Drew Carey*

By working faithfully eight hours a day you may eventually get to be boss and work twelve hours a day. – *Robert Frost*

The closest a person ever comes to perfection is when he fills out a job application form. - *Stanley Randall*

Be so good they can't ignore you. - *Steve Martin*

Enemies

I did not attend his funeral, but I sent a nice letter saying I approved of it. - *Mark Twain*

You have enemies? Good. That means you've stood up for something, sometime in your life. – *Winston Churchill*

Forgive your enemies, but never forget their names. – *John F. Kennedy*

Choose your friends carefully. Your enemies will choose you. - *Yassir Arafat*

Always forgive your enemies – nothing annoys them so much. – *Oscar Wilde*

**My mother used to say that there are no strangers, only friends you haven't met yet. She's now in a maximum-security

twilight home in Australia. - *Dame Edna Everage*

The pen is mightier than the sword, if you shoot that pen out of a gun. – *Stephen Colbert*

Alcohol may be man's worst enemy. But the Bible says to love your enemy. – *Frank Sinatra*

You may be your worst enemy if you let your negative thoughts hold you back from opportunities. – *Anon.*

Dress well whenever you go out as a girl may meet a dashing stranger or her worst enemy. – *Anon.*

Environment

Our job is improving the quality of life, not just delaying death. - *Robin Williams*

We must stop and ask ourselves. How much clean air do we really need? – *Lee Iacocca*

What is the use of a house if you haven't got a tolerable planet to put it on? - *Thoreau*

Our modern industrial economy takes a mountain covered with trees, lakes, and running streams and transforms it into a mountain of junk, garbage, slime pits, and debris. - *Edward Abbey*

There's so much pollution in the air now that if it weren't for our lungs there'd be no place to put it all. – *Robert Orben*

The use of solar energy has not been opened up because the oil industry does not own the sun. – *Ralph Nader*

Not all chemicals are bad. Without chemicals such as hydrogen and oxygen, for example, there would be no way to make water, a vital ingredient in beer. - *Dave Barry*

It isn't pollution that's harming the environment. It's the impurities in our air and water that are doing it. – *Dan Quayle*

Thank God men cannot fly, and lay waste the sky as well as the earth. - *Thoreau*

There are no passengers on Spaceship Earth. We are all crew. - *Marshall McLuhan*

Sex is a part of nature. I go along with nature. - *Marilyn Monroe*

According to a survey in this weeks' Time magazine, 85% of Americans think global warming is happening. The other 15% work for the White House. - *Jay Leno*

Failure

A failure is like fertilizer; it stinks to be sure, but it makes things grow faster in the future. – *Denis Waitley*

Don't think about your errors or failures, otherwise you'll never do a thing. - *Bill Murray*

It is failure that gives you the proper perspective on success. - *Ellen DeGeneres*

Whenever you fail, always pick something up. - *Avery*

I have not failed. I've just found 10,000 ways that won't work. – *Thomas A. Edison*

If you have a flop movie, so what? And if you have a hit movie, it's 'so what,' too – it's on to the next movie. - *Eddie Murphy*

Trying is the first step toward failure. – *Homer Simpson*

The good thing about failure is that it is only temporary and the bad thing about winning is that it is only temporary. – *Anon.*

Failures are finger posts on the road to achievement. - *C.S. Lewis*

We are all failures - at least the best of us are. - *J.M. Barrie*

Family

The advantage of growing up with siblings is that you become very good at fractions. *— Robert Brault*

All happy families are alike; each unhappy family is unhappy in its own way. *- Leo Tolstoy , Anna Karenina*

Families are like fudge - mostly sweet, with a few nuts. *- Les Dawson*

The capacity for friendship is God's way of apologizing for our families. *- Jay McInerney*

One day you will do things for me that you hate. That is what it means to be family. *- Jonathan Safran Foer*

Families are messy. Immortal families are eternally messy. Sometimes the best we can do is to remind each other that we're related for better or for worse...and try to keep the maiming and killing to a minimum. - *Rick Riordan*

If minutes were kept of a family gathering, they would show that members not present and subjects discussed were one and the same. - *Robert Brault*

I grew up with six brothers. That's how I learned to dance -waiting for the bathroom. - *Bob Hope*

Girls! Never let an angry sister comb your hair. - *Patricia McCann*

**On the serious side, the greatest thing a father can do for his children is to respect the woman that gave birth to his children. It is because of her that you

have the greatest treasures in your life. You may have moved on, but your children have not. If you can't be her soulmate, then at least be thoughtful. Whom your children love should always be someone that you acknowledge with kindness. Your children notice everything and will follow your example. - *Shannon L. Alder*

Family: A social unit where the father is concerned with parking space, the children with outer space, and the mother with closet space. – *Evan Esar*

The advantage of having only one child is that you always know who did it. - *Erma Bombeck*

The great advantage of living in a large family is that early lesson of life's essential unfairness. - *Nancy Mitford*

In some families, please is described as the magic word. In our house, however, it was sorry. - *Margaret Laurence*

When everything goes to hell, the people who stand by you without flinching - they are your family. - *Jim Butcher*

A dog reflects the family life. Whoever saw a frisky dog in a gloomy family, or a sad dog in a happy one? Snarling people have snarling dogs, dangerous people have dangerous ones. - *Arthur Conan Doyle, The Casebook of Sherlock Holmes*

The story of my family. . .changes with the teller. - *Jennifer Haigh,*

Fashion

Clothes make the man. Naked people have little or no influence on society. - *Mark Twain*

A fashion designer friend told me, "Don't wear what fashion designers tell you to wear. Instead, wear what they wear. – *Tina Fey*

Q. Where did all your money go? A. I'm wearing it. – *Anon.*

Fashion is what you're offered four times a year by designers. And style is what you choose. – *Lauren Hutton*

One is never over-dressed or under-dressed in a Little Black Dress. – *Karl Lagerfeld*

Can you please spell Gabbana? – *Andrea Sachs*

I have always believed that fashion was not only to make women more beautiful, but also to reassure them, give them confidence. – *Yves Saint Laurent*

She can beat me, but she cannot beat my outfit. – *Rihanna*

Girls do not dress for boys. They dress for themselves, of course, and each other. If girls dressed for boys, they'd just walk around naked at all times. – *Betsey Johnson*

Don't be into trends. Don't make fashion own you, but you decide what you are, what you want to express by the way you dress and the way you live. – *Gianni Versace*

Over the years, I have learned that what is important in a dress is the woman who is wearing it. – *Yves Saint Laurent*

Whoever said that money can't buy happiness, simply didn't know where to go shopping. – *Bo Derek*

Flattery

Flattery is like cologne water, to be smelt, not swallowed. – *Josh Billings*

Crocodiles are easy. They try to kill and eat you. People are harder. Sometimes they pretend to be your friend first. – *Steve Irwin*

Imitation is the sincerest form of flattery. – *Anon.*

Flattery is like chewing gum. Enjoy it but don't swallow it. - *Hank Ketcham*

Although a skillful flatterer is a most delightful companion if you have him all to yourself, his taste becomes very doubtful when he takes to

complimenting other people. - *Charles Dickens*

A fool flatters himself, a wise man flatters the fool. - *Edward Bulwer-Lytton*

Flattery is telling the other person precisely what he thinks about himself - *Dale Carnegie*

No one ever told me I was pretty when I was a little girl. All little girls should be told they're pretty, even if they aren't. - *Marilyn Monroe*

Food

Food is like sex: When you abstain, even the worst stuff begins to look good. - *Beth McCollister*

I always cook with wine. Sometimes I even add it to the food. - *W.C. Fields*

If this is coffee, please bring me some tea; but if this is tea, please bring me some coffee. - *Abraham Lincoln*

Knowledge is knowing a tomato is a fruit; wisdom is not putting it in a fruit salad. – *Miles Kington*

Vegetables – what food eats before it becomes food. - *David Weber*

Water is the most essential element in life, because without it you can't make coffee. — *Karen Salmansohn*

The most remarkable thing about my mother is that for thirty years she served the family nothing but leftovers. The original meal has never been found. *- Calvin Trillin*

Nouvelle Cuisine, roughly translated, means I can't believe I paid ninety-six dollars and I'm still hungry. *- Mike Kalin*

A slice of pie without cheese is like a kiss without a squeeze. *- Stephen King*

At a formal dinner party, the person nearest death should always be seated closest to the bathroom. *- George Carlin*

Do you know what breakfast cereal is made of? It's made of all those little

curly wooden shavings you find in pencil sharpeners! - *Roald Dahl*

Strength is the capacity to break a chocolate bar into four pieces with your bare hands - and then eat just one of the pieces. - *Judith Viorst*

My favorite flavor of cake is more. – *Anon.*

Clean eating journal. Day 1: I am a goddess and my body is a temple. Day 3: Well, that was fun. – *Anon.*

Pull up a chair. Take a taste. Come join us. Life is so endlessly delicious. - *Ruth Reichl*

Free Speech

Never confuse your right to say what you believe with a right to never be disagreed with and ridiculed for saying what you believe. - *Ricky Gervais*

Some tourists think Amsterdam is a city of sin, but in truth it is a city of freedom. And in freedom, most people find sin. - *John Green*

I prefer someone who burns the flag and then wraps themselves up in the Constitution over someone who burns the Constitution and then wraps themselves up in the flag. – *Molly Ivins*

Free speech means the right to shout "theatre" in a crowded fire. – *Abbie Hoffman*

A man may be a pessimistic determinist before lunch and an optimistic believer in the will's freedom after it. – *Aldous Huxley*

Who is more to be pitied, a writer bound and gagged by policemen or one living in perfect freedom who has nothing more to say? - *Kurt Vonnegut*

The things you own end up owning you. It's only after you lose everything that you're free to do anything. - *Chuck Palahniuk*

I felt the most free when I didn't have a penny. – *Mike Tyson*

The truth will set you free. But not until it is finished with you. - *David Foster Wallace*

Friends

Friends are people who know you really well and like you anyway. - *Greg Tamblyn*

You can make more friends in two months by becoming interested in other people than you can in two years by trying to get other people interested in you. - *Dale Carnegie*

A Crusader put a chastity belt on his wife and gave the key to his best friend for safekeeping, in case of his death.

He had ridden only a few miles away when his friend, riding hard, caught up with him, saying 'You gave me the wrong key! – *Old joke*

It is one of the blessings of old friends that you can afford to be stupid with them. - *Ralph Waldo Emerson*

A true friend stabs you in the front. - *Oscar Wilde*

Friendship is like peeing on yourself: everyone can see it, but only you get the warm feeling that it brings. - *Robert Bloch*

There are three faithful friends, an old wife, an old dog, and ready money. - *Benjamin Franklin*

An old friend will help you move. A good friend will help you move a dead body. - *Jim Hayes*

A friend is one who knows us but loves us anyway. - *Fr. Jerome Cummings*

The imaginary friends I had as a kid dropped me because their friends thought I didn't exist. - *Aaron Machado*

True friends are like diamonds - bright, beautiful, valuable, and always in style.
-Nicole Richie

Future

The best thing about the future is that it comes one day at a time. – *Abraham Lincoln*

If you want to make God laugh, tell him about your future plans. - *Woody Allen*

Intelligent life? The surest sign that intelligent life exists elsewhere in the universe is that it has never tried to contact us. – *Bill Watterson*

I dream of a better tomorrow, where chickens can cross the road and not be questioned about their motives. – *Ralph Waldo Emerson*

The world is full of magical things patiently waiting for our wits to grow sharper. – *Bertrand Russell*

That's the funny thing about life. We're rarely aware of the bullets we dodge. The just-misses. The almost-never-happened. We spend so much time worrying about how the future is going to play out and not nearly enough time admiring the precious perfection of the present. – *Lauren Miller*

There's no present. There's only the immediate future and the recent past. – *George Carlin*

This was my attempt to deter cold callers: "There's no past, there's no future, just one pulsating present... Please leave your message after the tone." – *Bill Bailey*

Gay

Do we have to worry about who's gay and who's straight? Can't we just love everybody and judge them by the car they drive? - *Ellen DeGeneres*

We had gay burglars the other night. They broke in and rearranged the furniture. – *Robin Williams*

A lot of gay men stay in the closet because they are interested in fashion. - *George Carlin*

I'm thinking - I'm homophobic; I hear it all the time.

"Dave, you're probably gay."

"What?"

"Well, you talk about being gay, so you probably are gay! You probably secretly want to have sex with another man!"

And I say, "Listen, voice in my head...I do not."

"How do you know you wouldn't like it? How do you know you wouldn't love it?"

I know I wouldn't like it or love it, because one time...during a terrible gardening accident, I sat on a cucumber - times. It happens. You never see it on ER, but it's happening. Every 8 minutes out there, someone is sitting on a cucumber, or papaya if you live in Hawaii. We need emergency programs. If that ever happens, you need two things and two things quick: a pair of ice tongs, and a friend that can keep a secret. Preferably your midget friend. Cause nobody believes a midget until it's too late.

Cucumber up a man's ass? Is that where the treasure is? Well then lead me, into your midget world! – *Dave Attell*

My cousin's gay, he went to London only to find out that Big Ben was a clock. – *Rodney Dangerfield*

I think that gay marriage is something that should be between a man and a woman. - *Arnold Schwarzenegger*

We're told to go on living our lives as usual, because to do otherwise is to let the terrorists win, and really, what would upset the Taliban more than a gay woman wearing a suit in front of a room full of Jews? - *Ellen DeGeneres*

I wish that every other guy was gay. In other words, 50% of men would be gay - think about the leverage that would create in your relationship. – *Dov Davidoff*

I have no idea why gay men love me, but I would have to assume it's because they know how much I love the gays! Everyone needs a good gay man in their life. – *Chelsea Handler*

The only way woman can truly be completely satisfied is to get herself four different men--an old one, an ugly one, a Mandingo, and a gay guy. – *Steve Harvey*

Genius

But the fact that some geniuses were laughed at does not imply that all who are laughed at are geniuses. They laughed at Columbus, they laughed at Fulton, they laughed at the Wright Brothers. But they also laughed at Bozo the Clown. – *Carl Sagan*

What the world needs is more geniuses with humility; there are so few of us left. – *Oscar Levant*

I can stand brute force, but brute reason is quite unbearable. There is something unfair about its use. It is hitting below the intellect. – *Oscar Wilde*

A genius is one who shoots at something no one else can see and hits it. – *Anon.*

Men of genius are rarely much annoyed by the company of vulgar people. - *Samuel Taylor Coleridge*

The secret of genius is to carry the spirit of the child into old age, which means never losing your enthusiasm. *- Aldous Huxley*

Genius is eternal patience. *– Michelangelo*

There's a fine line between genius and insanity. I have erased this line. *- Oscar Levant*

Happiness

Happiness is waking up, looking at the clock and finding that you still have two hours left to sleep. - *Charles M. Schultz*

The thing everyone should realize is that the key to happiness is being happy by yourself and for yourself. - *Ellen DeGeneres*

Happiness is an imaginary condition, formerly attributed by the living to the dead, now usually attributed by adults to children, and by children to adults. – *Thomas Szasz*

It isn't what you have or who you are or where you are or what you are doing that makes you happy or unhappy. It is what you think about it. - *Dale Carnegie*

Grudges are a waste of perfect happiness. Laugh, apologize, and let go of what you can't change. - *George Carlin*

I think the saddest people always try their hardest to make people happy. Because they know what it's like to feel absolutely worthless and they don't want anybody else to feel like that. – *Robin Williams*

Happiness is when what you think, what you say, and what you do are in harmony. - *Mahatma Gandhi*

To be stupid, selfish, and have good health are three requirements for happiness, though if stupidity is lacking, all is lost. - *Gustave Flaubert*

Hate

I told my psychiatrist that everyone hates me. He said I was being ridiculous – everyone hasn't met me yet. - *Rodney Dangerfield*

I know that there are people who do not love their fellow man, and I hate people like that! – *Tom Lehrer*

Haters are just confused admirers because they can't figure out the reason why everyone loves you. – *Jeffree Star*

Hating people is like burning down your own house to get rid of a rat. - *Henry Emerson Fosdick*

Health

The only way to keep your health is to eat what you don't want, drink what you don't like, and do what you'd rather not. - *Mark Twain*

Health nuts are going to feel stupid someday, lying in hospitals dying of nothing. - *Redd Foxx*

Older people shouldn't eat health food. They need all the preservatives they can get. - *Robert Orben*

The bad part about old age is decreasing health. The good part about old age is that it doesn't last that long. – *Anon.*

A hospital is no place to be sick. - *Samuel Goldwyn*

If I knew I was going to live this long, I'd have taken better care of myself. - *Mickey Mantle*

Don't eat anything your great-grandmother wouldn't recognize as food.

Eat food. Not too much. Mostly plants. – *Professor Michael Pollan*

Eat clean, stay fit, and have a burger to stay sane. – *Gigi Hadid*

When you start eating food without labels, you no longer need to count the calories. – *Amanda Kraft*

Heaven

Go to Heaven for the climate, Hell for the company. - *Mark Twain*

When I die, I hope to go to Heaven, wherever the hell that is. - *Ayn Rand*

To be in hell is to drift: to be in Heaven is to steer. - *George Bernard Shaw*

Socialism only works in two places: Heaven where they don't need it and hell where they already have it. - *Ronald Reagan*

Tears are often the telescope by which men see far into heaven. - *Henry Ward Beecher*

Humor

You grow up the day you have your first real laugh at yourself. - *Ethel Barrymore*

Analyzing humor is like dissecting a frog. Few people are interested, and the frog dies of it. – *E. B. White*

Humor is also a way of saying something serious. - *T.S. Eliot*

Always laugh when you can. It is cheap medicine. - *Lord Byron*

Don't take life too seriously. Punch it in the face when it needs a good hit. Laugh at it. And Laugh a lot. Never go a day without laughing at least once. - *Colleen Hoover, Slammed*

Trouble knocked at the door, but, hearing laughter, hurried away. – *Benjamin Franklin*

He who laughs last didn't get the joke. – *Charles de Gaulle*

Common sense and a sense of humor are the same thing, moving at different speeds. A sense of humor is just common sense, dancing. – *William James*

The secret source of humor itself is not joy, but sorrow. There is no humor in heaven. - *Mark Twain*

When people are laughing, they're generally not killing each other. - *Alan Alda*

If you want to make an audience laugh, you dress a man up like an old lady and push him down the stairs. If you want to make comedy writers laugh, you push an actual old lady down the stairs. - *Tina Fey*

Everybody laughs the same in every language because laughter is a universal connection. – *Yakov Smirnoff*

And we should consider every day lost on which we have not danced at least once. And we should call every truth false which was not accompanied by at least one laugh. - *Friedrich Nietzsche*

Against the assault of laughter, nothing can stand. - *Mark Twain*

Laughter is the sun that drives winter from the human face. - *Victor Hugo*

Good humor is a tonic for mind and body. It is the best antidote for anxiety and depression. It is a business asset. It attracts and keep friends. It lightens human burdens. It is the direct route to serenity and contentment. - *Greenville Kleisser*

Laughter heals all wounds, and that's one thing that everybody shares. No matter what you're going through, it makes you forget about your problems. I think the world should keep laughing. - *Kevin Hart*

Laughter is America's most important export. - *Walt Disney*

And keep a sense of humor. It doesn't mean you have to tell jokes. If you can't think of anything else, when you're my age, take off your clothes and walk in front of a mirror. I guarantee you'll get a laugh. — *Art Linkletter*

If you wish to glimpse inside a human soul and get to know the man, don't bother analyzing his ways of being silent, of talking, of weeping, or seeing how much he is moved by noble ideas; you'll get better results if you just watch him laugh. If he laughs well, he's a good man...All I claim to know is that laughter is the most reliable gauge of human nature. — *Feodor Dostoyevsky*

Insanity

The only mystery in life is why the kamikaze pilots wore helmets. - *Al McGuire*

I don't go crazy. I am crazy. I just go normal from time to time. *– Anon.*

Roses are red, violets are blue, I'm schizophrenic, and so am I. *– Oscar Levant*

I tell you, in this world, being a little crazy helps to keep you sane. *- Zsa Zsa Gabor*

I don't suffer from insanity. I enjoy every minute of it. *- Sherrilyn Kenyon in "Dance with the Devil"*

My psychiatrist told me I was crazy, and I said I want a second opinion. He said okay, you're ugly too. – *Rodney Dangerfield*

When we remember we are all mad, the mysteries disappear, and life stands explained. - *Mark Twain*

Nobody realizes that some people expend tremendous energy merely to be normal. - *Albert Camus*

I'm crazy, I'm nuts. Just the way my brain works. I'm not normal. I think differently. - *Justin Bieber*

Irony

I went to a meeting for premature ejaculators. I left early. - *Jack Benny*

Religion. It's given people hope in a world torn apart by religion. - *Jon Stewart*

We learn from experience that men never learn anything from experience. – *George Bernard Shaw*

I think the saddest people always try their hardest to make people happy. - *Robin Williams*

I see Atheists are fighting and killing each other again, over who doesn't believe in any God the most. - *Ricky Gervais*

If there is anything the nonconformist hates worse than a conformist, it's another nonconformist who doesn't conform to the prevailing standard of nonconformity. – *Bill Vaughan*

New Scientist magazine reported that in the future, cars could be powered by hazelnuts. That's encouraging, considering an eight-ounce jar of hazelnuts costs about nine dollars. Yeah, I've got an idea for a car that runs on bald eagle heads and Faberge eggs. - *Jimmy Fallon*

I celebrated Thanksgiving in an old-fashioned way. I invited everyone in my neighborhood to my house, we had an enormous feast, and then I killed them and took their land. - *Jon Stewart*

Half our life is spent trying to find something to do with the time we have rushed through life trying to save. – *Will Rogers*

My greatest hero is Nelson Mandela. What a man. Incarcerated for 25 years, he was released in 1990 and he hasn't reoffended. I think he's going straight, which shows you prison does work. - *Ricky Gervais*

The irony of all this is that the internet was supposed to be created to save us time. – *Anon.*

Most all people lie one time or another, but the irony of it all is that most all people don't like being lied to. – *Anon.*

It's ironic that women spend more time thinking about what men are thinking more than men think. – *Anon.*

Know It Alls

People who think they know everything are a great annoyance to those of us who do. – *Isaac Asimov*

You cannot be anything if you want to be everything. – *Solomon Schechter*

I'm astounded by people who want to 'know' the universe when it's hard enough to find your way around Chinatown. - *Woody Allen*

Nothing is as frustrating as arguing with someone who knows what he's talking about. - *Sam Ewing*

When I'm right, no one remembers, when I'm wrong, no one forgets. – *Anon.*

If know it all's really do know everything, then then should know how annoying they are. – *Anon.*

Nobody knows what God's plan is for your life, but a whole lot of people will guess for you if you let them. - *Shannon L. Alder*

Those who always know what's best are a universal pest. - *Piet Hein*

The smaller your reality the more convinced you are that you know everything. – *Thomas Campbell*

It's arrogant to be certain of anything. The world is a complex place and only idiots, or assholes think they know it all.
- Lisa Gardner

Lawyers

When you go into court you are putting your fate into the hands of twelve people who weren't smart enough to get out of jury duty. – *Norm Crosby*

I learned law so well, the day I graduated I sued the college, won the case, and got my tuition back. - *Fred Allen*

A verbal contract isn't worth the paper it's written on. – *Samuel Goldwyn*

The good lawyer is not the man who has an eye to every side and angle of contingency, and qualifies all his qualifications, but who throws himself on your part so heartily, that he can get you out of a scrape. - *Ralph Waldo Emerson*

To me, a lawyer is basically the person that knows the rules of the country. We're all throwing the dice, playing the game, moving our pieces around the board, but if there is a problem the lawyer is the only person who has read the inside of the top of the box. - *Jerry Seinfeld*

There are more lawyers in just Washington, D.C. than in all of Japan. They've got about as many lawyers as we have sumo-wrestlers. - *Lee Iacocca*

Arguing with a lawyer is not the hardest thing in the world; not arguing is. - *Raheel Farooq*

Laziness

You'll never be as lazy as whoever named the fireplace. – *Jason on Twitter*

I'm lazy. But it's the lazy people who invented the wheel and the bicycle because they didn't like walking or carrying things. *- Lech Walesa*

People say nothing is impossible, but I do nothing every day. *- A.A. Milne, from Winnie-the-Pooh*

Everybody seems to think I'm lazy, but I don't mind. I think they're crazy with running everywhere at such a speed until they find there's no need. *- John Lennon*

Lies

A lie gets halfway around the world before the truth has a chance to get its pants on. - *Winston S. Churchill*

I always tell the truth, even when I lie. *– Al Pacino*

Lies are like cockroaches for everyone you discover there are thousands more hidden. *– Gary Hopkins*

I'm not upset that you lied to me, I'm upset that from now on I can't believe you. - *Friedrich Nietzsche*

The best lies about me are the ones I told. - *Patrick Rothfuss, The Name of the Wind*

Life

Do not take life too seriously. You will never get out of it alive. - *Elbert Hubbard*

Life would be tragic if it weren't funny. - *Stephen Hawking*

I think I've discovered the secret of life - you just hang around until you get used to it. - *Charles Schulz*

Some days you're the dog; some days you're the hydrant. – *Anon.*

In three words I can sum up everything I've learned about life: it goes on. - *Robert Frost*

If you're not having fun, you're doing something wrong. -*Groucho Marx*

(Repeated from the Irony section) **Half our life is spent trying to find something to do with the time we have rushed through life trying to save**. – *Will Rogers*

Life is like a taxi. The meter keeps on running whether you are getting somewhere or just standing still. – *Lou Erickson*

Life is not measured by the number of breaths we take, but by the moments that take our breath away. - *George Carlin*

I live a little bit on the seat of my pants, I try to be alert and available for life to

happen to me. We're in this life, and if you're not available, the sort of ordinary time goes past and you didn't live it. But if you're available, life gets huge. You're really living it. - *Bill Murray*

If life was fair, Elvis would be alive, and all the impersonators would be dead. - *Johnny Carson*

Life is a sexually transmitted disease. – *R. D. Laing*

Follow your passion. Stay true to yourself. Never follow someone else's path unless you're in the woods and you're lost, and you see a path. By all means, you should follow that. - *Ellen DeGeneres*

When I hear somebody sigh, 'Life is hard,' I am always tempted to ask, "Compared to what?" – *Sydney J. Harris*

Life moves pretty fast. If you don't stop and look around once in a while, you could miss it. – *John Hughes*

Everything happens for a reason. But sometimes the reason is that you're stupid and you make bad decisions. *Marion G. Harmon*

Life is hard; it's harder if you're stupid. – *John Wayne*

My focus is to forget the pain of life. Forget the pain, mock the pain, reduce it. And laugh. - *Jim Carrey*

When you're in jail, a good friend will be trying to bail you out. A best friend will be in the cell next to you saying, 'Damn, that was fun'. - *Groucho Marx*

Life is so damn short. For f*ck's sake, just do what makes you happy. - *Bill Murray*

Life is short. If you doubt me, ask a butterfly. Their average life span is a mere five to fourteen days. - *Ellen DeGeneres*

We've had some fun tonight - considering we're all gonna die someday. - *Steve Martin*

The secret of life is honesty and fair dealing. If you can fake that, you've got it made. - *Groucho Marx*

On the other side, some people say life is short and that you could get hit by a bus at any moment and that you have to live each day like it's your last.

Bullshit. Life is long. You're probably not gonna get hit by a bus. And you're gonna have to live with the choices you make for the next fifty years. - *Chris Rock*

The road to success is dotted with many tempting parking spaces. – *Will Rogers*

Enjoy life. Have fun. Be kind. Have worth. Have friends. Be honest. Laugh. Die with dignity. Make the most of it. It's all we've got. - *Ricky Gervais*

Love

Love is an irresistible desire to be irresistibly desired. – *Robert Frost*

We're all a little weird. And life is a little weird. And when we find someone whose weirdness is compatible with ours, we join up with them and fall into mutually satisfying weirdness — and call it love — true love. – *Robert Fulghum*

Love is a fire. But whether it is going to warm your hearth or burn down your house, you can never tell. - *Joan Crawford*

My friends tell me I have an intimacy problem. But they don't really know me.
- *Garry Shandling*

Obviously, if I was serious about having a relationship with someone long-term, the last people I would introduce him to would be my family. - *Chelsea Handler*

I love you. You annoy me more than I ever thought possible. But I want to spend every irritating minute with you.
– Anon.

You've gotta dance like there's nobody watching,

Love like you'll never be hurt,

Sing like there's nobody listening,

And live like it's heaven on earth.

- William W. Purkey

You know you're in love when you can't fall asleep because reality is finally better than your dreams. - *Dr. Seuss*

Man's Best Friend

According to a new survey, 90% of men say their lover is also their best friend. Which is really kind of disturbing when you consider man's best friend is his dog. – *Jay Leno*

Do not make the mistake of treating your dogs like humans or they will treat you like dogs. – *Martha Scott*

Outside of a dog, a book is man's best friend. Inside of a dog it's too dark to read. - *Groucho Marx*

I wonder if other dogs think poodles are members of a weird religious cult. - *Rita Rudner*

If there are no dogs in heaven, then when I die, I want to go where they went. – Will Rodgers

I've seen a look in a dogs' eyes, a quickly vanishing look of amazed contempt. – *John Steinbeck*

My dog winks at me sometimes... And I always wink back just in case it's some kind of code. – *Anon*

Every boy should have two things: a dog, and a mother willing to let him have one. - *Anon*

Marriage

My wife Mary and I have been married for forty-seven years and not once have we had an argument serious enough to consider divorce; murder, yes, but divorce, never. *– Jack Benny*

Happy is the man who finds a true friend, and far happier is he who finds that true friend in his wife. *- Franz Schubert*

What a kid I got, I told him about the birds and the bees, and he told me about the butcher and my wife. *- Rodney Dangerfield*

In my house I'm the boss, my wife is just the decision maker. *- Woody Allen*

We always hold hands. If I let go, she shops. - *Henny Youngman*

I've had bad luck with both my wives. The first one left me and the second one didn't. - *Patrick Murray*

An archaeologist is the best husband any woman can have; the older she gets, the more interested he is in her. - *Agatha Christie*

Marriage has no guarantees. If that's what you're looking for, go live with a car battery. - *Erma Bombeck*

**Marriage is a 24-hour job. You get married, you're no longer an individual. You can't do nothing by yourself when you get married. Everything is a team effort. 'Us', 'we', 'let's', honey, come on partner. You can't do nothing by yourself.

Kevin: Baby I'm gonna be right back I'm going to the store.

Wife: Well, wait, let me get my coat.

Kevin: Bit___, it's right there on the corner. I just wanna get some chips. I ain't going to sleep with nobody. - *Kevin Hart*

You can only offend me if you mean something to me. - Chris Rock

A successful marriage requires falling in love many times, always with the same person. - *Mignon McLaughlin*

My brother is gay, and my parents don't care, as long as he marries a doctor. - *Elayne Boosler*

Before you marry a person, you should first make them use a computer with slow Internet service to see who they really are. - *Will Ferrell*

By all means, marry. If you get a good wife, you'll become happy; if you get a bad one, you'll become a philosopher. - *Socrates*

Before marriage, a man declares that he would lay down his life to serve you; after marriage, he won't even lay down his newspaper to talk to you. – *Helen Rowland*

We sleep in separate rooms, we have dinner apart, we take separate vacations – we're doing everything we can to keep our marriage together. – *Rodney Dangerfield*

My wife is my soul mate. I can't imagine being without her. -*Matt Damon*

They say marriages are made in Heaven. But so is thunder and lightning.– *Clint Eastwood*

Marriage is like mushrooms: we notice too late if they are good or bad. – *Woody Allen*

My wife gets all the money I make. I just get an apple and clean clothes every morning. - *Ray Romano*

Men marry women with the hope they will never change. Women marry men with the hope they will change. Invariably they are both disappointed. – *Albert Einstein*

I live by my own rules as long as it's reviewed, revised, and approved by my wife... but still my own. – *Si Robertson*

The best way to get most husbands to do something is to suggest that perhaps they're too old to do it. *- Anne Bancroft*

You know what's funny? I don't ever feel the need to escape. I have a strong marriage. I like my life. You hear about these guys having midlife crises - I don't see that happening to me. *- Harry Connick, Jr.*

Materialism

Money won't buy happiness, but it will pay the salaries of a large research staff to study the problem. – *Bill Vaughan*

Money is not the most important thing in the world. Love is. Fortunately, I love money. – *Jackie Mason*

Whoever said money can't buy happiness didn't know where to shop. – *Gertrude Stein*

Many wealthy people are little more than janitors of their possessions. - *Frank Lloyd Wright*

There are only two tragedies in life: one is not getting what one wants, and the other is getting it. - *Oscar Wilde*

Why is there so much month left at the end of the money? – *John Barrymore*

I think everybody should get rich and famous and do everything they ever dreamed of so they can see that it's not the answer. - *Jim Carrey*

Trying to be happy by accumulating possessions is like trying to satisfy hunger by taping sandwiches all over your body. *-George Carlin*

Men

Men are like shoes. Some fit better than others. And sometimes you go out shopping and there's nothing you like. And then, as luck would have it, the next week you find two that are perfect, but you don't have the money to buy both. – *Janet Evanovich*

The only time a woman really succeeds in changing a man is when he is a baby. – *Natalie Wood*

For most men, life is a search for the proper Manila envelope in which to get themselves filed. - *Clifton Fadiman*

Men are simple things. They can survive a whole weekend with only three things: beer, boxer shorts and batteries for the remote control. - *Diana Jordan*

When I eventually met Mr. Right I had no idea that his first name was Always.
– Rita Rudner

A man is already halfway in love with any woman who listens to him. -
Brendan Francis

A woman without a man is like a fish without a bicycle. - Gloria Steinem

When a man opens a car door for his wife, it's either a new car or a new wife.
– Prince Philip

See, the problem is that God gives men a brain and a penis, and only enough blood to run one at a time. - Robin Williams

Behind every successful man is a woman, behind her is his wife. – *Groucho Marx*

Don't keep a man guessing too long – he's sure to find the answer somewhere else. – *Mae West*

Men want the same thing from their underwear that they want from women: a little bit of support, and a little bit of freedom. *-Jerry Seinfeld*

A successful man is one who makes more money than his wife can spend. A successful woman is one who can find such a man. – *Lana Turner*

**Here's all you have to know about men and women: women are crazy, men are stupid. And the main reason women are crazy is that men are stupid. - *George Carlin*

Only one man in a thousand is a leader of men – the other 999 follow women. - *Groucho Marx*

The true man wants two things: danger and play. For that reason, he wants woman, as the most dangerous plaything. - *Friedrich Nietzsche*

Never trust a man with a penis. *Darynda Jones, Third Grave Dead Ahead*

Mistakes

Learn from the mistakes of others. You can never live long enough to make them all yourself. - *Groucho Marx*

Laughing at our mistakes can lengthen our own life. Laughing at someone else's can shorten it. – *Cullen Hightower*

I'm sorry, if you were right, I'd agree with you. – *Robin Williams*

If you could kick the person in the pants responsible for most of your trouble, you wouldn't sit for a month. – *Theodore Roosevelt*

To err is human, but to really foul things up you need a computer. – *Paul R. Ehrlich*

The man who smiles when things go wrong has thought of someone to blame it on. – Robert Bloch

I have learned from my mistakes, and I am sure I can repeat them exactly. – Peter Cook

It's only when you look at an ant through a magnifying glass on a sunny day that you realize how often they burst into flames. - Harry Hill

I was born to make mistakes, not to fake perfection. – Drake

**Human beings, who are almost unique in having the ability to learn from the experience of others, are also

remarkable for their apparent disinclination to do so. – *Douglas Adams*

I'm selfish, impatient and a little insecure. I make mistakes, I am out of control and at times hard to handle. But if you can't handle me at my worst, then you sure as hell don't deserve me at my best. - *Marilyn Monroe*

If people refuse to look at you in a new light and they can only see you for what you were, only see you for the mistakes you've made, if they don't realize that you are not your mistakes, then they have to go. - *Steve Maraboli*

Never interrupt your enemy when he is making a mistake. - *Napoleon Bonaparte*

Mothers

I've never wrestled a rabid raccoon on speed, but I have tried removing a splinter from the foot of a hysterical four-year-old. – *Anon.*

An excerpt from "When God Created Mothers"

When the Good Lord was creating mothers, He was into His sixth day of "overtime" when the angel appeared and said. "You're doing a lot of fiddling around on this one."

And God said, "Have you read the specs on this order? She has to be completely washable, but not plastic. Have 180 moveable parts...all replaceable. Run on black coffee and leftovers. Have a lap that disappears when she stands up. A kiss that can cure anything from a broken leg to a disappointed love affair. And six pairs of hands."

The angel shook her head slowly and said. "Six pairs of hands.... no way."

It's not the hands that are causing me problems," God remarked, "it's the three pairs of eyes that mothers have to have."

That's on the standard model?" asked the angel.

God nodded. "One pair that sees through closed doors when she asks, 'What are you kids doing in there?' when she already knows. Another here in the back of her head that sees what she shouldn't but what she has to know, and of course the ones here in front that can look at a child when he goofs up and say. 'I understand and I love you' without so much as uttering a word."

"God," said the angel touching his

sleeve gently, "Get some rest tomorrow..."

"I can't," said God, "I'm so close to creating something so close to myself. Already I have one who heals herself when she is sick...can feed a family of six on one pound of hamburger...and can get a nine-year-old to stand under a shower."

The angel circled the model of a mother very slowly. "It's too soft," she sighed.

But tough!" said God excitedly. "You can imagine what this mother can do or endure."

"Can it think?"

"Not only can it think, but it can reason and compromise," said the Creator.

Finally, the angel bent over and ran her finger across the cheek. There's a leak," she pronounced. "I told You that You

were trying to put too much into this model."

It's not a leak," said the Lord, "It's a tear."

What's it for?"

It's for joy, sadness, disappointment, pain, loneliness, and pride."

"You are a genius," said the angel.

Somberly, God said, "I didn't put it there." — *Erma Bombeck. "When God Created Mothers"*

Motivation

People often say that motivation doesn't last. Well, neither does bathing – that's why we recommend it daily. – *Zig Ziglar*

Nothing is impossible, the word itself says "I'm possible! – *Audrey Hepburn*

I went to a bookstore and asked the saleswoman where the Self-Help section was. She said if she told me it would defeat the purpose. - *Dennis Miller*

Don't be too concerned about bad decisions. Bad decisions make good stories. – *Ellis Vidler*

Leadership is the art of getting someone else to do something you want done

because he wants to do it. – *Dwight D. Eisenhower*

We don't have to be defined by the things we did or didn't do in our past. Some people allow themselves to be controlled by regret. Maybe it's a regret, maybe it's not. It's merely something that happened. Get over it. - *Pittacus Lore*

It's only after you've stepped outside your comfort zone that you begin to change, grow, and transform. - *Roy T. Bennett*

Sometimes you just have to put on lip gloss and pretend to be psyched. - *Mindy Kaling*

Music

After I saw Jimmy (Hendrix) play, I just went home and wondered what the f**k I was going to do with my life. - *Jeff Beck*

I've been imitated so well I've heard people copy my mistakes. - *Jimi Hendrix*

Talking about music is like dancing about architecture. – *Steve Martin*

All music is folk music. I ain't never heard a horse sing a song. - *Louis Armstrong*

All the good music has already been written by people with wigs and stuff. - *Frank Zappa*

I don't know anything about music. In my line you don't have to. - *Elvis Presley*

I never had much interest in the piano until I realized that every time I played, a girl would appear on the piano bench to my left and another to my right. - *Duke Ellington*

Nothing soothes me more after a long and maddening course of pianoforte recitals than to sit and have my teeth drilled. — *George Bernard Shaw*

I love Wagner, but the music I prefer is that of a cat hung up by its tail outside a window and trying to stick to the panes of glass with its claws. — *Charles-Pierre Baudelaire*

Offended

Just because you're offended, doesn't mean you're right. - *Ricky Gervais*

You found it offensive? I found it funny. That's why I'm happier than you. - *Ricky Gervais*

It's okay if you don't like me. Not everyone has good taste. – *Anon.*

If you find me offensive. Then I suggest you quit finding me. – *Anon.*

If you're offended by my opinions, you should hear the ones I keep to myself – *Anon.*

Old Age

"**Life begins at 40 – but so do fallen arches, rheumatism, faulty eyesight, and the tendency to tell a story to the same person, three or four times.** – *Helen Rowland*

Age is an issue of mind over matter. If you don't mind, it doesn't matter. – *Mark Twain*

When I die, I want to die like my grandfather who died peacefully in his sleep. Not screaming like all the passengers in his car. – *Will Rogers*

Inflation for seniors is when you pay fifteen dollars for the ten-dollar haircut you used to get for five dollars when you had hair. – *Sam Ewing*

When I was a boy, the Dead Sea was only sick. – *George Burns*

You know you're getting old when you get that one candle on the cake. It's like, 'See if you can blow this out.' - *Jerry Seinfeld*

You know you're getting old when you stoop to tie your shoelaces and wonder what else you could do while you're down there. – *George Burns*

As you get older three things happen. The first is your memory goes, and I can't remember the other two. – *Norman Wisdom*

A stockbroker urged me to buy a stock that would triple its value every year. I

told him, "At my age, I don't even buy green bananas." – *Claude Pepper*

My doctor told me that jogging could add years to my life. I think he was right. I feel ten years older already. – *Milton Berle*

Medium age: One of the many things nobody ever tells you about middle age is that it's such a nice change from being young. - *Dorothy Canfield Fisher*

Age is strictly a case of mind over matter. If you don't mind, it doesn't matter. - *Jack Benny*

I was thinking about how people seem to read the Bible a whole lot more as they get older; then it dawned on me –

they're cramming for their final exam. – *George Carlin*

I am an old man and have known a great many troubles, but most of them never happened. – *Mark Twain*

If you live to be one hundred, you've got it made. Very few people die past that age. – *George Burns*

My grandmother started walking five miles a day when she was sixty. She's ninety-seven now, and we don't know where the hell she is. – *Ellen DeGeneres*

I intend to live forever. So far, so good. – *Steven Wright*

Always go to other people's funerals, otherwise they won't come to yours. – *Yogi Berra*

If any of you cry at my funeral, I'll never speak to you again. – *Stan Laurel*

Age is not how old you are but how many years you've had fun. – *Matt Maldre*

I've reached the age where the little voice inside me used to say, "You shouldn't have said that," to "What the hell, let's see what happens." – *Anon.*

Opportunities

Life opens up opportunities to you, and you either take them or you stay afraid of taking them. - *Jim Carrey*

The early bird gets the worm, but the second mouse gets the cheese. – *Steven Wright*

Opportunity is missed by most people because it is dressed in overalls and looks like work. – *Thomas A. Edison*

If a window of opportunity appears, don't pull down the shade. - *Tom Peters*

If opportunity doesn't knock, build a door. - *Milton Berle*

Optomism

An optimist is someone who falls off the Empire State Building, and after 50 floors says, "So far so good!" – *Anon.*

A pessimist sees the difficulty in every opportunity; an optimist sees the opportunity in every difficulty. - *Winston S. Churchill*

We are all in the gutter, but some of us are looking at the stars. - *Oscar Wilde*

How wonderful it is that nobody needs to wait a single moment before starting to improve the world. - *Anne Frank*

To think well of yourself and to proclaim this fact to the world, not in loud words but great deeds.

To live in faith that the whole world is on your side so long as you are true to the best that is in you." - *Christian D. Larson, Your Forces and How to Use Them*

"We'll never survive!"

"Nonsense. You're only saying that because no one ever has." – *William Goldman*

As long as there was coffee in the world, how bad could things be? – *Cassandra Clare*

The average pencil is seven inches long, with just a half-inch eraser – in case you thought optimism was dead. – *Robert Braul*

Overweight

Inside me there's a thin person struggling to get out, but I can usually sedate him with four or five cupcakes. – *Bob Thaves*

I'm in shape. Round is a shape. – *George Carlin*

My favorite machine at the gym is the vending machine. – *Caroline Rhea*

Thin people are beautiful, but fat people are adorable. - *Jackie Gleason*

Fat-bashing in all its varied forms– criticism, exclusion, shaming, fat talk, self-deprecation, jokes, gossip, bullying–is one of the last acceptable

forms of prejudice. From a very young age, before they can walk away or defend themselves, women are taught that they are how they look, not what they do or what they know. - *Robyn Silverman, Good Girls Don't Get Fat: How Weight Obsession Is Messing Up Our Girls and How We Can Help Them Thrive Despite It*

Fat is your friend. The brain thrives on a fat-rich, low-carbohydrate diet. - *David Perlmutter*

My fat never made me less money - *Dolly Parton*

I try to avoid things that make me fat like scales, mirrors, and photos. – *Anon.*

Parents

When I was a kid my parents moved around a lot, but I always found them. – *Rodney Dangerfield*

As a kid my parents would send me out to collect for UNICEF, on Halloween which just screws up the whole holiday. You're wearing a costume and people are giving you pennies and you're going, "Well, give me some candy, you f**k."

And the grown-ups tell you, "Absolutely not. You've got your pennies. Now go build a village, you little sh*t."

It still brings a tear to my eye. – *Lewis Black*

My parents were very protective. I couldn't even cross the street without them getting all excited, and... placing bets. – *Emo Phillips*

Grandparents are there to help the child get into mischief they haven't thought of yet. - *Gene Perret*

I'm the youngest, too. When you're the youngest of a big family, people are like, "You're the baby, you're spoiled!"

The fact of the matter is, when you're the youngest of a big family, by the time you're a teenager, your parents are insane. You're like, "Hey, I'm going roller-skating-"

"You're not going roller-skating or you'll end up pregnant like your sister. Why don't you smoke pot and become a lawyer?" – *Jim Gaffigan*

And me having kids, with my family history? My mom: mentally ill, shot and killed her last husband. My father: six ex-wives, four heart attacks. Both of my parents think alcohol is a food group. - *Christopher Titus*

I could tell that my parents hated me. My bath toys were a toaster and a radio.
- Rodney Dangerfield

My nickname is 'Mom', but my full name is 'Mom Mom Mom Mom Mom Mom'. – Anon.

Buying your kid a goldfish is a great way to teach them about responsibility for 24-36 hours. -Conan O'Brien

An hour with your grandchildren can make you feel young again. Anything longer than that, and you start to age quickly. - Gene Perret

Perfection

It will never be perfect, but perfect is overrated. Perfect is boring on live TV. - *Tina Fey*

Perfection is not attainable, but if we chase perfection, we can catch excellence. - *Vince Lombardi*

A perfection of means, and confusion of aims, seems to be our main problem. - *Albert Einstein*

The essence of being human is that one does not seek perfection. - *George Orwell*

**I think it is interesting and funny to see all the cracks and all the flaws and all

the moments that are not perfect. - *Clemence Poesy*

Just because nobody complains doesn't mean all parachutes are perfect. - *Benny Hill*

There are two kinds of perfect: The one you can never achieve, and the other, by just being yourself. - *Lauren King*

I abhor the idea of a perfect world. It would bore me to tears. - *Shelby Foote*

Pessimists

A pessimist is a man who thinks everybody is as nasty as himself and hates them for it. - *George Bernard Shaw*

A pessimist is a person who has had to listen to too many optimists. – *Don Marquis*

Life is as tedious as a twice-told tale vexing the dull ear of a drowsy man.

Or a poor player that struts and frets his hour on the stage signifying nothing. - *William Shakespeare*

My pessimism extends to the point of even suspecting the sincerity of other pessimists. – *Jean Rostand*

Phones

People are prisoners of their phones... that's why it's called a "cell" phone. – *Anon.*

Technology can be our best friend, and technology can also be the biggest party pooper of our lives. It interrupts our own story, interrupts our ability to have a thought or a daydream, to imagine something wonderful, because we're too busy bridging the walk from the cafeteria back to the office on the cell phone. - *Steven Spielberg*

You know, a cell phone's like a guy; if you don't plug him in every night, charge him good, you got nothing at all.- *Catherine Coulter, Tail Spin*

Cell phones are so convenient that they're an inconvenience. - *Haruki Murakami*

Right, my phone. When these things first appeared, they were so cool. Only when it was too late did people realize they are as cool as electronic tags on remand prisoners. - *David Mitchell*

Cell phones these days keep getting thinner and smarter... people the opposite. – *Anon.*

Ode to Cell Phone: Cell Phone, if you didn't light up and buzz so many times to tell me you had a low battery, you wouldn't have died so fast! - *Anon.*

Politics

Politics gives guys so much power that they tend to behave badly around women. And I hope I never get into that. - *Bill Clinton*

A politician is someone who promises a bridge even when there's no water. — *Gregory David Roberts*

I believe in an America where millions of Americans believe in an America that's the America millions of Americans believe in. That's the America I love. - *Mitt Romney*

It would be nice to spend billions on schools and roads, but right now that money is desperately needed for political ads. – *Andy Borowitz*

I've always said that in politics, your enemies can't hurt you, but your friends will kill you. - *Ann Richards*

Political correctness is tyranny with manners. – *Charlton Heston*

True terror is to wake up one morning and discover that your high school class is running the country. – *Kurt Vonnegut*

They misunderestimated me. – *George W. Bush*

To those of you who received honors, awards and distinctions, I say well done. And to the C students, I say you, too, can be president of the United States. – *George W. Bush*

If 'con' is the opposite of pro, then isn't Congress the opposite of progress? - *Jon Stewart*

When I was a boy, I was told that anybody could become President. I'm beginning to believe it. – *Clarence Darrow*

Everything is changing. People are taking the comedians seriously and the politicians as a joke. - *Will Rogers*

Those who survived the San Francisco earthquake said, "Thank God, I'm still alive." But, of course, those who died, their lives will never be the same again.
- *Barbara Boxer, U.S. Senator*

Procrastination

Procrastinate now, don't put it off. - *Ellen DeGeneres*

The greatest thief this world has ever produced is procrastination, and he is still at large. – *Josh Billings*

Never put off till tomorrow what you can do the day after tomorrow. – *Mark Twain*

The words "If" and "When" were planted in the ground -- nothing grew. – *Old Proverb*

He who hesitates is last. - *Mae West*

When there is a hill to climb, don't think that waiting will make it smaller. – *Anon.*

Procrastination is like a credit card; it's a lot fun until you get the bill. - *Christopher Parker*

Procrastination always gives you something to look forward to. - *Joan Konner*

I'm going to stop putting things off, starting tomorrow! - *Sam Levenson*

The time you enjoy wasting is not wasted time. - *Bertrand Russell*

Things may come to those who wait, but only the things left by those who have done it already. - *Abraham Lincoln*

Psychics

Here's something to think about: How come you never see a headline like "Psychic Wins Lottery"? – *Jay Leno*

Predictions are difficult. Especially about the future. - *Yogi Berra*

I'm not telling you what to do, I'm just telling you what you're going to do. There's a difference. - *Jennifer Lynn Barnes*

I'm ADD and psychic. I know things ahead of time but lose track of which is which. - *S. Kelley Harrell*

Fear sees, even when eyes are closed. - *Wayne Gerard Trotman, Veterans of the Psychic Wars*

Ad: We are looking forward to welcoming talented magicians, clairvoyants, psychics and mediums for creative and highly paid work. The time and place you already know. – *Anon.*

I am a mind reader and very skilled at mind reading. Right now, I know what you're thinking - You don't believe me. – *Anon.*

Skeletons in the closet

If you can't get rid of the skeletons in your closet, you best teach them to dance. – *George Bernard Shaw*

Not many skeletons left in my closet because I invite them to dance all over the front room! - *John Schneider*

The self-righteous scream judgments against others to hide the noise of skeletons dancing in their own closets. - *John Mark Green*

If you could count the skeletons in my closet, under my bed and up under my faucet, then you would know I've completely lost it. Is he nuts? No he's insane! – *Eminem*

Sex

My best birth control now is just to leave the lights on. - *Joan Rivers*

The difference between sex and love is that sex relieves tension and love causes it. - *Woody Allen*

If you love something set it free, but don't be surprised if it comes back with herpes. – *Chuck Palahniuk*

I'm such a good lover because I practice a lot on my own. – *Woody Allen*

I don't have a dirty mind. I have a very creative sexy imagination. – *Anon.*

We were so loud having sex, even the neighbors had a cigarette. – *Anon.*

"I would rather cuddle then have sex."

Reply: I like your grammar! It shows perfect timing. – *Anon.*

It's not true that I had nothing on. I had the radio on. - *Marilyn Monroe*

Seems to me the basic conflict between men and women, sexually, is that men are like firemen. To men, sex is an emergency, and no matter what we're doing we can be ready in two minutes. Women, on the other hand, are like fire. They're very exciting, but the conditions have to be exactly right for it to occur. - *Jerry Seinfeld*

Sports

It's just a job. Grass grows, birds fly, waves pound the sand. I beat people up. – *Muhammad Ali*

Playing polo is like trying to play golf during an earthquake. - *Sylvester Stallone*

It's a round ball and a round bat, and you got to hit it square. - *Pete Rose*

If you make every game a life-and-death thing, you're going to have problems. You'll be dead a lot. - *Dean Smith*

**Rugby is a beastly game played by gentlemen; soccer is a gentleman's

game played by beasts; football is a beastly game played by beasts. - *Henry Blaha*

All hockey players are bilingual. They know English and profanity. - *Gordie Howe*

Pro football is like nuclear warfare. There are no winners, only survivors. - *Frank Gifford*

I've never lost a game I just ran out of time. - *Michael Jordan*

I finally made it to my first PGA Tournament by invitation. I was so nervous I hit my first drive off the first tee out of bounds. I reteed and hit my second drive even further out of bounds.

Then it got worse from there on. – *Anonymous PGA pro now working in a golf retail.*

The rules of soccer are very simple, basically it is this: if it moves, kick it. If it doesn't move, kick it until it does. - *Phil Woosnam*

Wrestling is ballet with violence. - *Jesse Ventura*

It's kind of funny, ability is what you're capable of doing, motivation determines what you do, but your attitude, believe it or not, determines how well you do it. - *Lou Holtz*

Teens

Wifi went down so I had to talk to my parents. They seem like nice people. – *Anon.*

Why do they rate a movie "R" for "adult language?" The only people I hear using that language are teenagers. – *Anon.*

Life is a process during which one initially gets less and less dependent, independent, and then more and more dependent. - *Mokokoma Mokhonoana*

When your children are teenagers, it's important to have a dog so that someone in the house is happy to see you. - *Nora Ephron*

Teenage girls are too caught up in being with a guy who's the best for everyone else and not the best for themselves. - *Anon.*

Prison for the crime of puberty -- that was how secondary school had seemed. - *David Brin, Earth*

There are just so many funny kids and teenagers. They're just not aware of how funny they are. - *Vanessa Bayer*

I love being in a public space where teenagers are talking. And the funny thing is that it hasn't changed that much. There's certainly slang that I'm not familiar with, but among the average teen, it's still the same. - *Marti Noxon*

When you are in your teenage years you are consciously experiencing everything for the first time, so adolescent stories are all beginnings. There are never any endings. - *Aidan Chambers*

We've told you many times not to do that and grounding you isn't enough punishment, so, we are very sorry, but we've decided you've got to be seen in public with us. – *Anon.*

Live your life like you are 80 years old looking back on your teenage years. - *Taylor Swift*

Truth

That's the other thing I learned that day, that the truth, however shocking or uncomfortable, in the end leads to liberation and dignity. - *Ricky Gervais*

Evening news is where they begin with 'Good evening', and then proceed to tell you why it isn't. – *Anon.*

It is hard to believe that a man is telling the truth when you know that you would lie if you were in his place. - *H. L. Mencken*

I never give them hell. I just tell the truth and they think it's hell. - *Harry S. Truman*

Always telling the truth is no doubt better than always lying, although equally pathological. - *Robert Brault*

Trust

Never trust people who smile constantly. They're either selling something or not very bright. - *Laurell K. Hamilton*

The best way to find out if you can trust someone is to trust them. – *Ernest Hemingway*

Trust yourself. You will always know more than what you think you know. – *Anon.*

In God we trust, all others we virus scan. – *Anon.*

Trust everybody but cut the cards. - *Finley Peter Dunne*

Women

The perfect accompaniment to a lovely dinner is not an ageless wine, but a beautiful woman. - *Anthony T. Hincks*

A woman is like a tea bag – you can't tell how strong she is until you put her in hot water. – *Eleanor Roosevelt*

I hate women because they always know where things are. – *Voltaire*

Feminine intuition is a fiction and a fraud. It is nonsensical, illogical, emotional, ridiculous, and practically foolproof. - *Harry Haenigsen*

The most terrifying thing any woman can say to me is "Notice anything different?" - *Mike Vanatta*

I do not spew profanities. I enunciate them clearly, like a fucking lady. – *Anon.*

Women are meant to be loved, not to be understood. – *Oscar Wilde*

There's treachery in her hips, rebellion in her heart and magic in her mind. - *Curtis Tyrone Jones*

Woman. She will never grow old; her heart is too beautiful. - *Nikki Rowe*

The problem with life is, by the time you can read women like a book, your library card has expired. - *Milton Berle*

Mind of engaging empathetic intellect is a true woman. A complex and lasting beauty. - *Richard L. Ratliff*

Scientists now believe that the primary biological function of breasts is to make men stupid. - *Dave Barry*

There are a number of mechanical devices which increase sexual arousal, particularly in women. Chief among these is the Mercedes-Benz 380SL convertible. - *P. J. O'Rourke*

America is a land where men govern, but women rule. - *John Mason Brown*

All women may not be beautiful, but every woman can look beautiful. - *Amit Kalantri*

A young woman stood before the railing, speaking to the reception clerk. Her slender body seemed out of all scale in relation to a normal human body; its lines were so long, so fragile, so exaggerated that she looked like a stylized drawing of a woman and made the correct proportions of a normal being appear heavy and awkward beside her. – *Ayn Rand*

There are only three things women need in life: food, water and compliments. - *Chris Rock*

When it comes to emotions, women know how to paint with the full set of

oils, while men are busy doodling with crayons. - *Hank Moody*

A woman's mind is cleaner than a man's: She changes it more often. – *Oliver Herford*

Man has his will, but woman has her way. – *Oliver Wendell Holmes Sr.*

Women are wiser than men because they know less and understand more. – *James Thurber*

Give me a woman who loves beer and I will conquer the world. – *Kaiser Wilhelm II, German Emperor*

She wore a plain gray suit; the contrast between its tailored severity and her appearance was deliberately exorbitant—and strangely elegant. She let the fingertips of one hand rest on the railing, a narrow hand ending the straight imperious line of her arm. She had gray eyes that were not ovals, but two long, rectangular cuts edged by parallel lines of lashes; she had an air of cold serenity and an exquisitely vicious mouth. Her face, her pale gold hair, her suit seemed to have no color, but only a hint, just on the verge of the reality of color, making the full reality seem vulgar. A man stood still, because he understood for the first time what it was that artists spoke about when they spoke of beauty. - Ayn Rand

Sometimes people are beautiful. Not in looks. Not in what they say. Just in what they are. - *Markus Zusak*

Work

A boss on vacation is the most cost-effective measure. Everybody in the office has a vacation at the cost of one.
– *Thibaut*

It's true hard work never killed anybody, but I figure, why take the chance? – *Ronald Reagan*

My grandfather once told me that there were two kinds of people: those who do the work and those who take the credit. He told me to try to be in the first group; there was much less competition.
– *Indira Gandhi*

I'd rather have 1% of the effort of 100 men than 100% of my own effort. – *J. Paul Getty*

Most people work just hard enough not to get fired and get paid just enough money not to quit. - *George Carlin*

Some people see things that are and ask, Why? Some people dream of things that never were and ask, Why not? Some people must go to work and don't have time for all that. - *George Carlin*

If you don't know what to do with many of the papers piled on your desk, stick a dozen colleagues initials on them and pass them along. When in doubt, route. - *Malcolm S. Forbes*

I love deadlines. I love the whooshing noise they make as they go by. - *Douglas Adams, The Salmon of Doubt*

World

I think we need more love in the world. We need more kindness, more compassion, more joy, more laughter. I definitely want to contribute to that. - *Ellen DeGeneres*

Don't go around saying the world owes you a living. The world owes you nothing. It was here first. - *Mark Twain*

Funny is the world I live in. You're funny, I'm interested. You're not funny, I'm not interested. - *Jerry Seinfeld*

What the world really needs is more love and less paperwork. - *Pearl Bailey*

Richard Pryor introduced me to the world of the inner city, and the urban world, and did it hysterically. My favorite comedian, even though we

work 180 degrees differently, but funny is funny is funny. - *Bob Newhart*

I look at the world and I find the funny in it, because there's funny in everything. No matter how ugly it may be, there's a funny way to look at it. - *Charlie Murphy*

Never doubt that a small group of thoughtful, committed, citizens can change the world. Indeed, it is the only thing that ever has. - *Margaret Mead*

Personally, I don't think there's intelligent life on other planets. Why should other planets be any different from this one? - *Bob Monkhouse*

People are illogical, unreasonable, and self-centered. Love them anyway.

If you do good, people will accuse you of selfish ulterior motives. Do good anyway.

If you are successful, you will win false friends and true enemies. Succeed anyway.

The good you do today will be forgotten tomorrow. Do good anyway.

Honesty and frankness make you vulnerable. Be honest and frank anyway.

The biggest men and women with the biggest ideas can be shot down by the smallest men and women with the smallest minds. Think big anyway.

People favor underdogs but follow only top dogs. Fight for a few underdogs anyway.

What you spend years building may be destroyed overnight. Build anyway.

People really need help but may attack you if you do help them. Help people anyway.

Give the world the best you have, and you'll get kicked in the teeth. Give the world the best you have anyway. — *Kent M. Keith, The Silent Revolution: Dynamic Leadership in the Student Council*

Forget champagne and caviar – Taste the world instead! – *Hostelgeeks*

Peace, which costs nothing, is attended with infinitely more advantage than any victory with all its expense. - *Thomas Paine*

There is perhaps no better demonstration of the folly of human conceits than this distant image of our tiny world. To me, it underscores our responsibility to deal more kindly with one another, and to preserve and cherish the pale blue dot, the only home we've ever known. - *Carl Sagan, Pale Blue Dot: A Vision of the Human Future in Space.*

About the Editors

Team Golfwell and Bruce Miller, J.D. are bestselling authors who live in New Zealand.

Thank you very much for your interest in our book and we hope you enjoyed it and had a laugh or two.

If you liked our book and have the time, we would appreciate your leaving a very brief review on Amazon, Goodreads and/or Barnes & Noble.

Thank you again very much!

Sincerely,

TeamGolfwell.com & Bruce Miller, J.D.

Printed in Great Britain
by Amazon